Süleyman

A Minute A Lifetime

November 2019

Süleyman Ergüçlü, was born in 1954 in the Yenicami area of the old town of Lefkoşa. In his lifetime; in 1958, at the age of 4, he met the tear gas of the British colonial soldiers; in 1963, when he was 9, he lost his father (Kara Yusuf), who was 47 when he died; the same year, 4 months later, he experienced the intercommunal fighting; in1969, at the age of 15 he joined the resistance organisation and became a Mujahid; in 1974, at the age of 20, he had to fight a war. He studied Computer Programming in London in early 70's. When he returned he joined the media sector and worked as a journalist for many years until he retired. In his career, he worked at the radio The Voice of Cyprus, Bayrak Radio and Television Corporation, and various newspapers. When he retired, he was the Editor in Chief of the Kıbrıs Media Group.

Süleyman Ergüçlü

suleyman@erguclu.eu

ISBN 978-9963-275-90-8

Introduction

Having completed my training as a computer programmer in England, I returned to Cyprus. My time in England passed under very difficult conditions. My mother, who was with me, was trying to help me financial y by sewing at home. I was also working out of school time. Our relatives in London were also helping. They welcomed and hosted us at their homes for a long time.

Maybe I could have stayed in London after my training but it seemed very difficult to engage in computer programming about which I was educated.

That was because the computer was a recent thing, and it was not widespread even in London. Therefore, if I stayed, I could have only been a worker at the manufacturing plant. For example during my training, I learnt how to do ironing very wel . I was the person making the first line to the newly sewed up pants at the factory of a businessman from Louroudjina (Luricina).

Moreover had I stayed there, I would not be serving the remaining time of my military service. Therefore, I would have been away from the dangerous environments in Cyprus. Yet, I did not prefer these, and as soon as my training was over, I came back to Cyprus. It was the end of the year 1973.

In Cyprus there was an irreplaceable absence for me. My grandmother (from my mother's side) Cemaliye Köroğlu, who had sent me off to London with tears in her eyes, was no longer among us. She had passed away while I was in London. And according to the information relayed to me, her final words were "my tall and handsome". She was using this expression to describe me. I was sick at heart. Very sad. The pain of losing her has never ceased.

My grandmother was a true and strongly dedicated Ottoman woman, and she used to believe that men were superior. For example, although I was only 9 years old, she used to think that I was the "head of the family" after we lost my father. She was frequently quarreling about this with my sisters. And at that very young age, I was exploiting this to the end. My mother used to get angry about the situation.

But now, she was not among us. My granny was not alive. I had to accommodate myself to the situation, and I did. I started looking for a job.

However, since computers were not widespread in those days, nobody was interested. However, I had to work to earn a living. First, I started working as an apprentice for a merchant. Later, I found a job to work as a technician at hosiery. A couple of months later, I decided to complete my remaining service as a mujahid .

I was sent to the Support Unit (Heavy Weapons Unit) that I had served as a student-mujahid until I went to England, and I began active duty. The company commander was my aunt's son Mehmet Ali Yıltay. Since I was a senior, they appointed me as the chief of the armory and storehouse.

15 July Greek coup

I am at Bayraktar Headquarters. A historical assemblage of buildings.

It was formerly the Turkish High School (Türk Lisesi). Subsequently, with the outbreak of the inter-communal events, this building was converted into a military quarter. The battalion known as the affiliated units was placed there.

The affiliated units consisted of the Marching Band Company, Quarter Support Company, and Support Company (Heavy Weapons Company). My duty was at the Support Company as a recoilless (57mm) gunman. Afterwards, the Company left the place and having stayed in the buildings of Yıldırım Company, located just outside Ortaköy, for a short time, they moved into the building which used to be the Greek Cypriot tobacco factory prior to 1963, and which is now the Turkish Cypriot Parliament. The Assembly Hall of the Parliament was, at that time, our dormitory. We were stationed in that building in 1974...

Our former headquarters, Bayraktar building was very special for me because my childhood passed there. When it was the High School, and I was a child, my deceased father Yusuf Salih (Kara Yusuf) was working as a sports teacher there, and he was the dorm manager. Our house was on the street just behind that building.

My favorite person at school was, of course, Ali Aylakçı because he was the canteen man. And he had the chocolates.

Year 1958-59...
With my father Yusuf Salih (Kara Yusuf) in the yard of the High School...

It was 15 July 1974, and I was attending a training on "Small Troop Leadership" at Bayraktar. If I successful y completed the training, I would be a corporal. The training was proceeding but I was thinking about those old days.

The trainer was the Commander İbrahim Latif, who died a martyr in Lefkoşa shortly afterwards.

Suddenly, the gun shots began to be heard but they were silenced after a little while. We were all excited but commander İbrahim Latif told us that we will continue with the lecture. After a while the sounds of machine guns began to be heard again, and this time they did not go silent. Commander İbrahim Latif said; "Boys, everybody shall go back to their troops along the shortest route without panicking". But is it possible not to panic at all? We all began to run towards our troops, along the quite narrow streets of the old town Lefkoşa.

As I arrived in my unit, the company was preparing to move out to specific positions which had been determined in advance. Since ours was the heavy weapon company, it used to be distributed among the positions in various regions of Lefkoşa during war. I was responsible for the armory, and I had the key to the ammunition store. However, our Commander Mehmet Ali Yıltay had opened the ammunition store with his own key and distributed the guns.

I was the gunman of 57 mm recoilless gun but the commander told me to stay at the headquarters for the time being.

The Greek Cypriots were fighting among themselves. The coup d'état of 15 July that was aimed at overthrowing Makarios and annexing the island to Greece had started. The coup d'état was instigated by EOKA, the Greek Cypriot underground organization, with the support of the military junta in Greece.

The coup was going to fail due to the intervention by Turkey on 20 July, and the coming of the Turkish soldiers to the island.

Year 1969...

With my friend Salim, at 57 mm Recoilless Gun (GTT) training...

In the meantime, the civilian personnel, who were to join us in case of fighting, had already started to arrive at the company, and they were waiting to be assigned a duty. The commanders were giving duties suitable for everybody.

I was distributing meals to our friends who were in various regions of Lefkoşa.

Wherever I go, I was hearing different things, and I was as confused about what was happening, just as everybody else was.

Once in a while, I was stopping by my mother, dropping by our home.

Our house was crowded as always. Our relatives and their relatives living in dangerous regions had altogether moved into our house. My deceased mother would hug me and cry each time she saw me. I told her that should she continue to cry each time she saw me, I would stop visiting her, and the poor woman started to gulp down her tears at that instance, and never showed that she was crying.

At the same time, the Greek Cypriots were fighting among themselves. With the support of the military junta in Greece, and the plotters in the administration, the President Archbishop Makarios was alleged to be overth-rown and killed. And Nikos Samson was declared as the new President. In the meantime, Makarios had escaped and went to Paphos, and was talking live on a radio, and was saying that he was alive: *"İme Makarios. Den ime negros, ime zondanos."* That is to say; "I am Makarios. I am not dead. I am alive."

We were waiting. Wondering where would this be arriving at. Our Commanders were saying "this time, they will definitely come", referring to the Turkish army. But we had doubts about that.

Besides the Turkish Cypriots leaders, the Greek Cypriot leader Makarios was also inviting the Guarantors, Turkey and the UK to do something about the coup d'état instigated by the third guarantor Greece.

The First Operation

And the night of 19 July. It was approximately 22:00. We were about to go to bed. It was just at that moment that we realized the Company Commander was in a rush, and shortly after we saw Mehmet Sedat, the Sancaktar (code name of regional commanders) of Lefkoşa, entering the headquarters in a hurry. We were also alarmed. The Commander said; "Boys, you shall immediately get to rest. Make all men rest as wel . Tomorrow, we will be running off our feet". One of us asked, "Sir, are they coming?" The Commander's reply was not very clear: "Probably yes this time". We were full of hope but we couldn't be sure. And we went to get some rest.

Next morning, we were waken up very early on the morning of 20 July.

Our Company Commander summoned and told me; "Go to the position area next to the coffee shop on the old wal s, behind Gençlik Gücü Sports Club in Çağlayan. Just wait there for further orders. Then, you will move further, to Ayios Kasiano. They are in need of an anti-tank weapon in that area. You are a recoilless gunman but you can also use a bazooka (rocket launcher). Take a 89 mm bazooka and one of the civilian personnel and go to the position. They will direct you from there."

I took a bazooka and 8 rockets from the armory, and businessman Hilmi Refik, a civilian support personnel who was present there and I went to the region where Gençlik Gücü (GG) sports club is situated.

We reached the position ordered by the Commander by climbing up the old walls of Lefkoşa behind GG. There was one A4 machinegun at the position. We were told to wait there.

Year 1974...

In the yard of the building – now the Parliament- with an 89 mm Rocket Gun (Bazooka)...

Ayios Kasiano School was further ahead of the position. Just next to it on the old wall were the Greek Cypriot positions located. There was also a coffee shop just behind the position that we were waiting at that time. Halide and Nahide sisters, who were operating the coffee shop, were doing their best to help us. They were serving us, the mujahids at the positions, the meals they cook themselves because they did not like the ones sent to us. One day I told them; "thank you very much but you will run out of food at home if you continue like this". The reply: "No problem. Then we will eat the soldier's meal". I thought to myself; 'That's how the Turkish Cypriots are' and I was proud.

We pretty much stood waiting in this position during the first operation. Then, at the interval between the two operations, we were sent to the position area just next to the Greek Cypriot Ayios Kasiano School, located further ahead. There, we were very close to the Greek Cypriot positions. And we were waiting.

An A4 machinegun and a Brengun were at hand in the position. I had an 89 mm bazooka. In addition to these, we all had guns such as Stenguns, Thompson or pistols. Hüseyin Moral was using the A4 machine gun.

In fact, he was not using; rather he was watching over it. There wasn't much action in this position during the first operation and in its aftermath until the second operation. There used to be only some small scale shootings from time to time.

During one of these small scale conflicts, Moral was by his gun, firing it aimed at the position across. We were under fire from the opposite side.

During these reciprocal shootings, a bullet coming from the opposite position passed through the loophole, hit a part on the A4 machine gun, bounced and fell on the ground. We were all petrified. Should that bullet slipped only a few millimeters, it would have hit Hüseyin Moral on the forehead. Luckily, nobody was hurt. But it got us all shocked. We were all sweating due to the hot weather as well as our excitement.

Shortly after, when we pulled ourselves together, I took the Brengun, and started firing. Soon, I felt a strong burning on my arm, where my right arm was resting on the table. I looked down and saw that a blank shel , which just dropped off the gun and which was very hot, rolled down and squashed in between my arm and table. However the blank shell was so hot that it burnt my arm and stuck into my arm. I hit the blank shell as soon as I saw it and it fell down. But my arm was quite burnt. There was great pain. My friends immediately cleaned the burnt location, put some crème on it and covered it with plasters. But the pain persevered. There was nothing to do except for waiting.

In the meantime, there was a small tree between the Greek Cypriot position, next to Ag. Kasiano School, and our position. The tree was small but it was a blinder to both Greek Cypriots and us.

We were unable to see the Greek Cypriots well when we were shooting, and the Greek Cypriots had the same problem. They couldn't see us well when they were shooting.

We could not destroy the tree no matter what we did. We dropped Molotov cocktail, it did not explode. One exploded but this time the tree did not burn.

The Greek Cypriots were watching while we were making these efforts.

They were not firing because they also wanted that small tree to be destroyed.

Just as these were happening, one of us from our position took a bottle of gasoline and a lighter, jumped over the position and went near the tree. Acting quickly, he poured the gasoline on the tree and burnt it. He then came back running and jumped into the position.

The Greek Cypriots just watched without any intervention as all of these happened. The small tree burst into flames and burnt down in a short time. After 5 or 10 minutes, the small tree was not located between the positions any longer, and now we could fire by directly seeing each other, in a more efficient way. From that time on, we were able to swear at each other by seeing each other, although through the loophole.

Now, we could say that swear word which also entailed religious elements, with greater pleasure and louder than ever. Whenever we used that foul language, the Greek Cypriots used to start firing immediately with the machine gun. Now, everybody was happier.

I, on the other hand, was sitting with a bandage on my arm, and waiting for the wound to heal as soon as possible. The wound was small and was not preventing me from doing anything but it was gently hurting and it needed to heal.

I was sitting with a bandage on my arm and I was thinking; if my mother saw me like this, with a bandage on my arm, she would definitely drop dead. Therefore, should such a circumstance arise where my mother would see me, I thought to myself, that bandage should absolutely be removed.

Mürüde hanım of the Köroğlu family

My mother, Mürüde Yusuf or Mürüde Köroğlu. I started thinking about her. One and the only daughter of the Köroğlu family which was one of the most wealthy and notable families of the country. The princess of Köroğlu family who used to live in a mansion located on the street that was given the name of the family, in Arabahmet quarter, which was the region where the rich used to live at the time, within the walled city of Lefkoşa; the owner of the Köroğlu farm in Lakatamia. Mürüde Hanım, the niece of Mrs. Akıle who was the wife of Ottoman Grand Vizier Cypriot Kamil (Kiamil) Pasha. She was raised enviably, and although it was the 1930's and 1940's, it was ensured that she received the best training.

And yet, Mürüde Hanım somehow meets Yusuf Salih (Kara Yusuf), who was exactly a man of the people, and they fall in love. The son of cook Salih dayı of Ayakebir (Dilekkaya) and Ms. İsmet of Kaymaklı; Kara Yusuf, having worked for the British army in Egypt as a sergeant sports trainer, returned to Cyprus and he wanted to marry Mürüde Hanım. The Köroğlu family strictly said "no" as a reply to this desire. However Mürüde Hanım told her family that she would marry the man she loved as she went through fire and water.

In those years, such a move would require immense courage and self-confidence.

All efforts of the family to dissuade their daughter from this passionate love yielded no result. Mürüde Hanım abandoned her family and married Yusuf Salih. That being the case, the family gave their consent; albeit unwillingly.

The 1940's...

My mother Mürüde Köroğlu and my father Yusuf Salih...

The young couple lived on the farm for a while after their marriage.

Thereafter, when Yusuf Salih was appointed as a teacher, they came to Lefkoşa and rented a house in Yenicami region. Mürüde Hanım could not even imagine the luxurious life she used to live until that day. From now on there would be no nannies and servants. Mürüde Hanım was financial y living under very different living conditions; however she was happy.

In the meantime Yusuf Salih was working as a physical training teacher at the High School, and later on he became an inspector at the Department of Education. At the same time, he was among the first scout leaders. He also took part in the establishment of the Turkish Resistance Organization (Türk Mukavemet Teşkilatı/TMT). He was the first Serdar (regional commander-in-chief) of Lefkoşa region.

On another note, Mehmet Ali Köroğlu, the father of Mürüde Hanım, had passed away, and Cemaliye Hanım, her mother, began living with Mürüde Ha-nım and Yusuf Salih. In the meantime, Köroğlu family had lost all their wealth and they had to sell the farm in Lakatamia and their assets in Arabahmet.

I was very happy with my grandmother, who was a full-blooded Ottoman woman, living with us. Because my granny Cemaliye, who loved me much, and who thought that I was superior to my two elder sisters, was with us. She used to tell my sisters openly; "You, pieces of girls, don't you understand? Süleyman is a man, he is a man. You will respect him..." These words used to enrage my sisters and make me very happy. My grandmother never liked my father as well , and she used to make that clear at every opportunity.

The year 1964-65…

My grandmother Cemaliye Köroğlu with my elder sisters Işıl, İsmet and I…

My grandmother was always taking care of me and she was protecting me from everybody (including my father). Whenever I did something wrong and my father wanted to punish me, my grandmother would stand in front of me and tell my father "just hit me instead of him". Of course my father would turn back and move away.

After some time, we moved out of our home in Yenicami, the house in which I was born, and moved into a house behind the building which was then the High School. We had both very good and very bad days in that house. We lived through the events in 1958 in that house. The events were happening just next to our home and I was 4 years old.

After a while, we moved to a house, which used to be a shop, situated on Polis Street behind the Courts. This house belonged to us. It was our property. It was not a rental as were the others. My mother and father purchased it by borrowing money.

Polis Street was situated just outside Samanbahçe. My father's father, my grandfather Salih was living in Samanbahçe and he used to own a very small market.

It was while we were living in this house that my father Kara Yusuf passed away from a heart attack in August 1963. In December of the same year, the inter-communal conflict began. And there came the ensuing troublesome years.

Mürüde Hanım, who was raised pampered and spoiled, was now faced with the harshest aspect of life. She lost her beloved husband; and she had to live under blockade in destitute with her three children in the war environment, and she also had to maintain her family.

And despite all difficulties, she carried on. She succeeded in getting my two elder sisters married, and educating me in England. But she suffered a lot.

She was overwhelmed.

The Second Operation

The heat of August of the year 1974 is as hot as hell. The asphalted worn out roads of the ancient, old Lefkoşa that witnessed many wars throughout history are red-hot. It is as if we are burning but we are keeping an eye on the opposite Greek Cypriot positions. The second operation has begun and Turkish soldiers are progressing along the north of the island. There was not much action in our positions during the first operation but it seems that the second operation will be exciting.

In any event, the second operation begun thrilled for me. Before the second operation, we were resting in turns in our positions in Ayios Kasiano.

Later that night, I was sleeping in a bedroom in the second floor of a very small old house just behind our position. I was sleeping in my clothing. My gun was beside me.

My friends woke me up at an early hour of the morning, and said; "c'mon wake up, the operation has started". In a matter of minutes I came through and woke up, and I started going down the stairs. Just as I walked down 3 or 5 steps, a big explosion was heard from the room which I slept in. Everywhere was crumbled into dust. A mortar shell had fallen down on the room where I had been sleeping.

Good God! If that happened just seconds ago, I would have been torn to pieces. I walked down running and waited. There were no further shootings or anything else.

After a while I went upstairs and saw that the bed I had just gone out was riddled, shattered, and the cottons of the mattress were scattered around.

The roof of the room had collapsed, and the fragmentation of the mortar shell was also reflected on the furnishing in the room. I went down to our position, thanking God that I narrowly escaped death by seconds.

We are on pins and needles. We wonder what is happening in our country, we are trying to get information; however all we can see is what we can see through the loophole.

On our heads are the steel helmets that the Turkish soldiers wear, and we are not very accustomed to them. It is unbearable in that heat but we are obliged to wear them. Because when Greek Cypriots see these helmets, they would supposedly think that the Turkish troops have gained ground so far. That's why we are wearing them.

It was midday. Doğan Akpınar, the Company Commander of the region where we were present, issued an order: "Rocket launcher (bazooka) team shall go and destroy the Greek positions in so-and-so location". The group referred to as the team consists of me, the marksman, and Ersin, the assistant marksman. Indeed I was a recoilless gunman but I was sent to use bazooka because there was a deadlock in finding someone who can use a bazooka. As both were anti-tank weapons, I was knowledgeable about bazookas.

We immediately pulled up stakes and went to the region. We passed along Tantin's Hamam (Turkish Bath) and walked towards Kara Baba. Those are in the region where I was born. We were walking and staring around. Soon after we passed by Kara Baba shrine, we reached our destination.

In general, it is in the same area like ours but it is an unfamiliar area for us. It was at a remoter point than our position in Ayios Kasiano. They showed a semi-demolished old building and said; "You will launch rocket from this building to the position across".

Ersin and I entered into the old building. The Greek Cypriot position was very close. However it was under machine gun fire from the position ahead of us, so that they would be distracted and would not notice us. And the Greek Cypriots were firing at the position which was next to us and which was firing at them.

Slowly, we made the arrangements. Ersin mounted a rocket to rocket launcher. Now it was up to me.

In order to launch the rocket, I must shoulder the rocket launcher, and I must rise up to my waist, then I must aim and fire. However since the distance is very close, the probability is very high that the Greek Cypriots would see me.

But there was nothing I could do.

So I shouldered my rocket launcher and stood up, and rapidly aiming, I pulled the trigger. Good heavens! The rocket didn't fire. I waited a while and pulled the trigger again. But no result... The rocket didn't fire!

Ersin and I knew very well that in such an incident the marksman should wait a minute (60 seconds) while standing still in his position. And we began to wait.

I am waiting, without moving, my upper body is exposed, and visible.

The Greek Cypriot position is approximately 30 meters ahead. They can see me at any moment and easily shoot me. However there is nothing to do. I must wait. And I waited. I waited with my eyes on the scope.

At that time I feel the amulet (charm) that was attached inside my shirt with a hook, on my left breast. The amulet prepared and attached by Hadji Nine (Ayşe hodja of Limassol).

Hadji Nine had said; "wear this", "if you wear this, the enemy will see you like a monster and will be afraid of you". Although I do not have much faith in such things, feeling it there put my mind at rest a bit.

Hadji Nine was our neighbor. She was living with her daughter aunty Havva on Mahmut Pasha Street. They were originally from Limassol. Hadji Nine was among the first sought-after people by anybody who wanted to get Mevlid (a ritual on death and grief) read in Lefkoşa.

She had known me since my childhood. It was immediately after 15 July and before 20 July that I visited home when my mother told me that Hadji Nine would like to see me. I instantly went to see her. I kissed her hand.

She held a sizable amulet in her other hand. She told me; "Come my son, look. There will be a war. You will be careful. Look, I am going to put this on you. You will never take it off. This protects the ones who fight for the right and justice. The enemy sees the one, who wears this on, as a monster and gets scared, so cannot do anything. God bless you", and she affixed the amulet with a hook inside my shirt's collar in a manner not disturbing me. I was very moved and happy. I promised not to take off the amulet, kissed her hands, and left there to go to the position.

The Greek Cypriots are still firing the adjacent position. They have not seen me yet. Thousands of thoughts pass through my mind in a flash. And untimely stories are crossing my mind. My whole life starts to flash before my eyes.

The events of 1958

1958 comes to my mind. The events of 27-28 January. The colonial British soldiers opened fire on the Turkish High School students, who were protesting, and some became martyrs. I was 4 years old at the time. I don't know if I real y remember or I think I remember because I heard the story from my mother and grandmother over and over again. Nevertheless, I remember the events and our experiences during those days.

I was very excited and blissful in those days. Our relatives and friends, living outside the walled city of Lefkoşa, came to our house which was a safer place. Our home was just next to the Selimiye square, and behind the building that used to be a High School at the time, and which is now the Ministry of Tourism. It was situated in the immediate northern part of the region known as Tahtakale, and it was one of the closest points of the Walled City to the Greek side; however it was still a safe place. My aunt's, Uncle Sami's family and some of their friends were all at our home. My poor mother and granny were busy, trying to accommodate that much people and to look after us.

On the upper floor of our home, uncle Şener's family (Rifat Şener) was living. Uncle Şener, Aunty Afet Hanım and their children. We were like a family. In particular; we were constantly with their children Ulus, Huriye and Baysal because our ages were very close.

My father was not around. My father Yusuf Salih (Kara Yusuf) was a physical education teacher in the High School; however as we learnt later on, he was, at the same time the Serdar (Yayla Beyi), that is to say, the regional commander-in-chief of Lefkoşa region of the Turkish Resistance Organization (TMT). Natural y, nobody there had known my father's connection with the TMT but everybody accepted that he was somewhere out there.

My elder sisters Işıl and İsmet and I were feeling uncomfortable, because we could not understand what was going on, but we were also happy about being together with our relatives. My elder sister Işıl was aware of the events because she was a little bit older than we were; but İsmet and I could not understand anything.

Despite the efforts of the British soldiers and police to prevent, some students from the high school just next to our home went to Sarayönü (Atatürk Square) and they were protesting. Despite the British used tear gas and opened fire, the students staged their demonstration.

However, there were martyrs, and my nephew İbrahim was among them. Somehow, all such information used to reach our home, and it caused tension, stress and fear among the folks at home.

In the meantime, some tension was rising between the Greek Cypriots and Turkish Cypriots in. EOKA was active in the Greek Cypriot side, and TMT was active on our side. Everybody was tense, everybody was disturbed, and everybody was scared. We, the children, were trying to understand what was happening.

In such cases, I used to run to the arms of my grandmother and take refuge. Granny Cemaliye used to enfold me in her arms and say; "son, don't be afraid. Nothing will happen". But I can't help it. I was scared. Nevertheless, I was a child, and when my peers called me to play, I was forgetting my fears.

Nevertheless, everybody at home was nervous, tense and scared. What scared them most was the uncertainty. "What is going to happen now? What will the Greek Cypriots do? How will the British react?" That is to say uncertainty in short.

Year 1964-65...

At a young age, the guns were our most joyous toys, and we were imitating our elder brothers.

The guns coming for TMT

I keep waiting with the bazooka on my shoulder. Ersin is not moving.

When the time comes, he will remove the rocket which failed and mount a new rocket in its place, and he will softly touch my head. And I will fire again.

However, the time that we need to wait is not passing.

I am scared that they can see me from the opposite position and shoot me. But I cannot do anything. Because if I move and if there is late ignition, the rocket will explode in our arms, and all of my friends in the position will die with me. So I keep waiting.

My life continues to flash before my eyes. Now, I remember the holidays that we used to spend with my family before 1963 in the 3 Miles beach located in the east of Girne, north of Kazaphani (Ozanköy) vil age. We were very happy there.

We used to go there every summer, late in the 50's and early in the 60's. A beautiful bay in the north of Kazaphani. Now it is a military area, and Cratos Hotel stands next to it. We were staying either at uncle Ömer's house or in a big scout's tent. Every summer Dr. Küçük and his family used to be there as well.

Osman Örek used to come with his family from time to time. Every day, at the café by the sea, they used to chat with my father, uncle Hasan, who was running the café, and with other people.

We, the children, were playing happily. Mehmet Küçük, son of Dr. Küçük, Ümit Serdaroğlu, son of uncle Hasan, my elder sisters Işıl and İsmet, and other children were enjoying the sea and holiday.

In the mean time, Dr. Küçük, with his usual humor, used to send me to Mr. Hasan, who was known as Hasanoz, and who was living in Küçük Su bay that was just ahead, and he wanted me to call him "Mr. Hasan Öz". I used to go with great eagerness and fulfill this request, and in exchange of the swear words that I hear from Hasanoz, Dr. Küçük would give me half a shilling.

Also an Armenian family used to come from time to time. They also had a child of our age. That he could speak Turkish while we were playing, would make us very happy; however we used to laugh at the way he pronounced some words. For example he used to say "gidek" instead of "gidelim" or "yiyek" instead of "yiyelim". So far so good but one day, when he said "bu köpek örek" pointing to a barking dog, we were all frightened to death. In his way of talking, it meant "this dog is barking", but literally it meant "this dog is Örek", which was an unintended insult at Mr. Örek.

The older children among us warned the child in this respect and told him to be careful.

At that time we did not know that the holiday in the 3 Miles beach was an operation of the TMT. Of course my mother knew it. But we were only able to learn about it when we grew up.

It seems that we used to go there not for holiday but we were keeping company to my father who was going there to receive the guns arriving secretly for the TMT from Turkey by way of sea. We, the family, were somehow camouflaging the gun case. My father, who was one of the high level authorities of the TMT, was taking the guns and delivering them to Lefkoşa.

And again, I am back to the reality. Ersin is not making a move. I have to keep waiting. And I wait. And the time hangs heavy on my shoulders.

End of the 1960's...
The years of being a Student- Mujahid

The death of my Father

Just opposite, the machine gun position ahead is under Greek Cypriot fire. They are also firing back. The Greek Cypriots have not noticed me yet. But they can, at any moment. There is nothing I can do. I keep on waiting. Then I remember the month of August of the year 1963; I remember my father who died prematurely at the age of 47, an age which could still said to be young.

The heat of August was as hot as hell. It was around 15:00. 18 August 1963.

Sunday. 6 days to turn nine years old. We are at our home on Polis Street behind the Courts. My father is doing some repairs in the house. He demolished something, and built something else.

That day, a boy from our street is being circumcised. For this reason, my mother sent me to buy a cake to the confectionery of Altan, whose shop was under the Plümer's apartment building on the old wal s, very close to our house. I went, murmuring under the blazing sun.

After I bought the cake, and just as I was leaving the shop, an ambulance came across the Ledra Palace, passed by us, got down from Kanlı Mescit (a small mosque) and stormed into the side streets of Lefkoşa.

My friend and I said; "Let's follow the ambulance", and we went down from the Kanlı Mescit, and ran towards my house which was not far. We arrived at my home and we were shocked.

Our house was crowded. The ambulance was in front of my house. I was perplexedly standing in the middle of the crowd that had gathered in front of the house. I do not know what happened to the cakes that I was holding.

And a stretcher was coming from the house. My father was lying in it, motion-less. I wanted to run to him. They wouldn't let me. They put him in the ambulance and took him away. Then one of the children called out to me: "Your father died". I did not believe.

In the mean time, after my father had been taken away, Özkan Gülok came. As soon as he got out of his car, before he could even understand what was happening, he shouted at the people who were present there; "Tell the coach (my father), we are being late... We are waiting for him... The team (Gençlik Gücü) is going to the training...", and after he mumbled such words, he learnt what had happened and he became shocked. The football team Gençlik Gücü had been waiting for my father, who was both the coach and the chairman of the club, so that they could go for training.

At home, my mother was having a nervous breakdown. There was commotion around. I was told that my father was only ill, and that he did not die.

And I believed, I do not know, probably I believed because I wanted to believe.

They took my two sisters and me away. Everybody was crying. We were bewildered.

I was told that my father had fallen sick and sent to England for treatment. I was not taken to the funeral of my father. I realized the truth. Nevertheless, I wanted to play this game; so I played it.

As part of this game, they threw the biggest birthday party for me, on 24 August, 6 days after the demise of my father. We had a lot of fun during the celebration held at the home of my uncle Macit Köroğlu, which was located on Tanzimat Street, on the old walls. All of my friends and the children of the family were there. And they were all playing the pretence game that my father was not dead.

And the game continued. Until the shock I experienced when I went to enroll in Atatürk Primary School in September. The teacher who was enrolling the students asked me whose son I was. I told him; "My father is an inspector at the Department of Education. Yusuf Salih". The teacher did not understand who my father was. Until, the teacher next to him said; "he is the son of our deceased Kara Yusuf". And there, the game was over. I came face to face with the truth. Kara Yusuf was "deceased". Earlier they were telling me a lie. Now I was faced with the truth. And I no longer had a "father".

Running, I went back to our home, and I yelled at the top of my voice to my mother; "mum, my father is dead". And at that instance, my mother burst into tears. Then she hugged me and we cried our hearts out. Granny Cemaliye tried to control us, tried to comfort us; as if it were possible. The death of my father was being lived over, as if it happened just at that moment, and all family was hit again.

Ultimately my mother gathered herself up, with the support of my grandmother, and got the situation under control and looked after us. The grief that she had to repress and endure in silence was indigestible; yet Müride Hanım of the Köroğlu family, that strong woman achieved that. She achieved for us.

This grief that she had to endure after she had lost her husband, who was only 47 years old, from a heart attack, and whom she had fallen in love with and married despite all the pressures and objections of the Köroğlu family that had been a wealthy and aristocrat family in the 1940's, it was a grief that was unbearable by a woman who was only 39 years old and had 3 children.

The events of 1963
A martyr - Aziz Güner

And again I am back in the real world. My eye is on the scope of the Bazooka, and I keep waiting. And I had a mental picture of the events of 1963 that took place four months after the demise of my father, and one memory in particular came to my mind.

It is the immediate aftermath of 21 December 1963. There is a massive crowd at our home situated on Polis Street within the walled city of Lefkoşa. Our relatives, friends, the neighbors of our relatives who considered that suburbs of Lefkoşa was not a safe place to be in, had abandoned their houses in regions such as Çağlayan and Kumsal, and came to our house.

We were approximately 30 people in that small house. The majority consisted of women and children, and there were a few old men. The youth were at the front line. Nobody knew their whereabouts or the things they do. There was a continuous noise of guns. Nobody knew what to do, nobody knew what would happen. We, the children, were only scared. My mother would not let me go outside. We were only hovering in the doorway, and trying to learn something from the passersby.

It was 22 or 23 December. The weather was quite cold. I was standing in front of the door and gazing at the people passing by. Then I saw him. He was coming from the direction of Deniz Bookshop. My Aziz Abi (abi meaning big brother), Aziz Güner.

There was a stubbly beard of a couple of days on his face which always used to be shaved. The unfailing smile on his face was also invisible. He was wearing a thick coat. And in his hand, he was carrying a Sten machine gun. He was walking very quickly.

He approached when he noticed me at the door. The smile was back on his face. He told me; "What are you doing here? Go inside". In the meantime, my mother also came to the door. After my mum and Aziz Abi talked a while, I asked "Aziz Abi, what is happening?" His answer was very clear and reassuring. He said; "Süleyman, don't be afraid, don't worry". Then he showed me the gun in his hand, and said; "We are very strong. Don't be afraid. We will stop the Greek Cypriots. Nobody would ever harm you". He was so sure of himself that this conversation relieved us all.

I do not remember whether it was that day or the next. We got the news. Aziz Güner and his friends were martyred during an operation in the vicinity of the flour plant. I was shocked. Aziz Güner was no longer alive. That Aziz Güner, who believed in himself, who was a reassuring person, was no longer among us.

There would be no smile on Aziz Güner's face any more.

Aziz Güner would no longer give me strength, and reassurance, and he would not show me the primitive gun in his hand and say, "We are strong". He would no longer be able to go to the Gençlik Gücü Sports Club and chat with his friends. He would not be with his family. He would not be able to open his store at nights to give melodica to the spoiled children.

Following the shock I had had when I lost my father 3-4 months earlier, this shock was too painful, too hard. I went outside running, without taking permission from my mother, and went running to Tekke Bahçesi which was in a close proximity to our home. The place which was converted into a martyrdom right off the bat. I was crying. But it did not matter because everybody was crying.

Hüseyin Dayı, who used to bury the martyrs in Tekke Bahçesi, was making his preparations. He was preparing to bury Aziz Güner. Crying, I stood in a corner and watched. And Hüseyin Dayı laid Aziz Güner to rest. For good. And Aziz Güner was not with us anymore.

I returned home with these feelings and started to live that extraordinary environment again. There was something that attracted my attention. Üstün and Mehmet cousins, two sons of my aunt Cemaliye, who were with us in 1958, were not with us this time.

I immediately asked; “Where are my cousins?” The answer was clear: “They are at the front line; they are defending, protecting us. Take it easy, and don’t be afraid. Your cousins are there.”

1969 – A student mujahid

Ersin is still not moving. I am standing in front of the enemy, with half of my body visible. My upper body is clearly visible and I have a huge 89 mm bazooka on my shoulder. They can easily see and shoot me. However, they are busy firing at the position just ahead of us. And I keep on waiting.

The day on which I first enrolled as a mujahid came to my mind. I was talking with Tayyip, the youngest son of aunt Hayriye. We were talking about the guys at our school, who were a couple of grades older than us, and that they were mujahids, and were making show of being mujahids. I remember them making fun of us when the alarm was given by saying "We are going. You wait here with the girls". And at that moment, in that place, we decided to be student mujahids. It was 1969. I was 15, and Tayyip was 16 years old.

We weren't going to ask our mothers because if we did, they would not give permission.

And with this determination, we went to the headquarters of the Affiliated Units, which was located within the walled city of Lefkoşa. The units were located in the neighborhood and building where my childhood had passed.

This was formerly the building of the High School, and my father Kara Yusuf was a teacher there.

One of the commanders of the unit was Soner Çuvalcıoğlu who was the husband of a cousin of mine, Naile. Tayyip and I directly headed for Soner Çuvalcıoğlu. Told him; "We want to be mujahids ". He immediately asked; "Do your mothers know this?" And we immediately lied there; "Of course they know. Can we ever do this without them knowing?" It was completely a lie. Neither my mother nor aunty Hayriye knew it. And Soner Çuvalcıoğlu said; "Alright", and having completed the required procedures, he assigned Tayyip to the Marching Band Company, and I was assigned to the Support (Heavy weapons) Company.

We had great trouble with our mums when we went home that day.

However I said "I was with Tayyip", and Tayyip said "I was with Süleyman", so we managed to break the ice a little. After hours of tension, they accepted the situation. It was followed by advices at length, and the preparations were made to send us off to military.

Our mothers were right; we had never been away from home until that day. We were very young then. But we were also right under the circumstances of those days. We were feeling obliged to do that. We had to defend ourselves, our families and our community.

Upon arriving at the company, and after I completed the registration works, they gave me a uniform. That made me very happy and honored. Despite I was only 15 years old; I was feeling like a grown up, a "man".

I was assigned as a 57 mm Recoilless Gunman (RCL) at anti-tank team, where Commander Şenol was the team commander. I had never seen or heard that gun. The RCL, which could be used on a tripod or on the shoulder, was one of the most effective heavy weapons of the time. They had many similarities with the rocket launchers (bazooka) in terms of their usage. The company was using heavy weapons therefore they were constantly at training.

Apart from the trainings, we were on guard duty. The student mujahids were going to school, getting training and keeping guard. When I was a novice at the company, I was sent to guard duty with another friend for a brief time so that I would learn. Afterwards, I started to keep guard alone.

Our guard posts were just next to the Martyrs' Monument (Şehitler Anıtı), and it was the front and back sides of the building we used to call Kırıkkale. It was named after the Kırıkkale Gun Factory in Turkey since gun maintenance and repair works were being made there. The description of the guard posts were "Kırıkkale Front" and "Kırıkkale Back". Kırıkkale Front guard was kept along the street going from the

Martyrs' Monument to Ledra Palace. Kırıkkale Back guard was kept at the side-street in the back.

Since we were along the main street during our Kırıkkale Front guard, we used to dress like military police, used to carry a pistol instead of a normal gun, and put on white helmet. Whereas during Kırıkkale Back, we were on guard in our normal uniforms with Thompson machine guns.

My school, then the English College, was the building just opposite our Company Headquarters. I was jazzed up when I went to school that day. I was showing off to friends. And there were different reactions from the teachers.

Turkish teachers were appreciating. Foreign teachers were feeling an affectionate pity and considering "a child at this age is obliged to be a soldier, to take a gun in his hand".

After I got accustomed to being a student mujahid and got in the mood of it, I started to exploit the situation in my favour. In particular, I was approaching the foreign teachers during exam periods and tell them "Teacher, those commanders are not helping us. Today we have your course's exam but they put me on guard last night until the morning, and I did not have the chance to study." Of course it was a lie. The reaction of the teacher would always be the same; "It does not matter my child. Just sit for the exam. Do as much as you can do. We will handle the rest."

I was doing just the opposite to the commanders. I was telling them, "Captain, those foreign teachers are not showing any sympathy. They are acting as if everything is normal, and they consider us as equals with other students. And we are always given guard duty at the company. We are unable to prepare for our exams." The commanders would always give the same reaction: "The student mujahids shall immediately be taken off the guard duty list. They will be provided with every opportunity to study during exam periods. We will reconsider the situation after the exams."

This scenario continued until our teacher, Engin Kemal (the Boxer) found out what was going on. The Boxer used to be one of the Commanders at our Company some time ago, and he knew every commander there. One day, he went to the Company to visit his old friends. During the course of their conversation, the subject came to the student mujahids. And it was only then that our tricks came forth. Thereupon, I was called by Şinasi Tekman hodja, the then principal of our school, and he dropped the subject with a soft verbal warning.

“According to me”

Time hangs heavy on my hands. My friend Ersin is still not moving. In the meantime, the opposite Greek Cypriot position and the one next to me are under heavy reciprocal gun fire. I have to stand still and continue waiting. And that’s what I do.

An experience I had with our Turkish- literature teacher Kemal Mehmet Ali (Mehmet Ali Aksay) comes to my mind. Kemal Hodja (teacher) used to love me because he used to be a student of my father, and also I was good at Turkish lesson and writing essays.

One day, the teacher asked us to write an essay for our homework. We wrote and gave it to our teacher. The following lecture, he read and marked our essays and gave them back. I got a good grade. After he had distributed everyone’s essays, he turned to me and said “Süleyman, can you please read the first paragraph of your essay”. I immediately read the paragraph consisting of three or four sentences at once.

“Yes”, said Kemal Hodja, “you are using the phrase ‘according to me’ at one point in your paragraph. Now, let’s make a small practice together. Where are we now? We are at our school, in Haydarpaşa quarter, within the walled city of Lefkoşa. Now, close your eyes, and go into the space. Dive into the depths of the universe.”

“Have you succeeded? Now, do you see the stars around you, and our planet Earth far away?”, and I say “Yes, teacher.”

“Alright, now slowly find our planet Earth and move towards it”; “Yes, teacher, I have done it.”

“Good, now, find our island, Cyprus, on the Earth, and descend towards it”, “Alright, teacher.”

“Now, find Lefkoşa in Cyprus, and find Haydarpaşa quarter and our school, and come to our classroom”; “I came teacher”.

“Süleyman, now you can open your eyes. You have been through the universe, and saw its extent and grandness. You have got the feeling of what that means. Then, you saw the place our planet Earth holds within this endlessness. Haven’t you Süleyman?”; “Yes, teacher, that was a breathtaking experience.”

“Now, tell me, then; who and what are ‘you’ to use the phrase ‘according to me’ with such an ease within such an endlessness and grandness. Children; these words are valid for all of you. You have to think four times when using words such as ‘I’ and ‘according to me’”

Of course, when the teacher finished, I was already distressed. To my surprise, we had to be very careful and calculate the matter in depth when using these words that we have been using carelessly and freely. After that day, this became a sort of rule for me.

Scout camp in Yağmuralan (Vroyisha)

I see small movements in the opposite position; I feel it but cannot understand what's going on. From time to time, fire is opened from the adjacent position to the one across, and the opposite position responds in the same manner. And I keep on waiting.

All of a sudden, 3-4 months that we spent in a mountain village known as Yağmuralan (Vroyişa) in Dillirga region in the year 1959-60 came to my mind.

My father pitched a scout camp there and he was training the villagers allegedly about scouting. It was the British era and the British security forces were closely following such issues.

In the camp, weapon training was being given to the villagers in fact, and it was not scouting. This was once again an operation of the Turkish Resistance Organization (TMT). And we were present there as a family, as a camouflage.

We were very happy there. The beautiful people of Dillirga were extra-ordinarily hospitable to us, just as they have always been to all their guests; and in particular they were spoiling me, as I was the youngest.

The villagers were speaking Greek as if it was their mother tongue, and particularly the older people preferred to use the Greek language as their normal daily language.

My father and mother, apart from training, that was the duty of TMT, were building close relationships with the villagers; approaching them with love, and the villagers were having strong liking for them.

I knew that there was a scout camp in the village but I did not know that there were underhand practices, and that weapon training was given in the guise of a scout camp.

And in this way, we continued until the camp time, the training was completed, and we left there with beautiful memories and delightful friendships.

Reward

And once again, I am back to the real life. I keep waiting. The time that I am required to wait is not up yet. The Greek Cypriots continue shooting at the adjacent position. And they strike back. And I wait. Once again, I am lost in the thought of the past.

I remember getting an award of 5 Cyprus Pounds, it was in 1969 or 70. I am a student mujahid. I was on the watch in Kırıkkale Front. Since the location was in the limelight, there wouldn't be many incidences, and the guard duties would come and go. I was around 16 years old. One night, at a late hour a car came, two people got out, and walked towards the gate of Kırıkkale.

Under such a condition, I should have taken my gun out and ask; "Stop, who is it?" However; I was excited, and I called out to the men; "Hey! Stop. You cannot go in there". One of the men told me; "Son, look, I am the new commander of this place. I forgot my newspapers inside. I will take them and get out. You can also come if you want to". His friend next to him was grumbling; "For god's sake, let it go, let's go".

I said; "No, you cannot enter". The man who said that he was the commander told me; "Son, I will take my newspapers and leave. Come with us and see. There is nothing wrong".

I was insisting, and saying; "No you cannot go in." The man accompanying him was still saying; "Never mind, let's go!"

That certain person, addressing me and a bit angry, asked; "Look here! You haven't even taken your gun out of its holster. What will you do, if I enter now?" That moment, I realized that the man was right. I immediately took my gun out and pointed it to the man. It was an old pistol, Takarof type.

In the meantime, his friend was still insisting; "Let it go! Let's go." The person who claimed to be the new commander, continued to talk. "You have drawn your gun but you have not set it. It will be useless in this way. Look, I am a soldier, and if I want, I can take that gun from you, and I will do whatever I want." I realized that the man was right again, and I immediately loaded the gun.

The friend of the commander said; "Okay. This is it. We are going" and he pulled away his friend. As the commander was leaving with his friend, addressing to me, he said; "You immediately call your commander, and tell him everything. Just wait and see", and they got in the car and pulled away.

I called the duty officer, chief sentry, whoever was there, and informed them. The common opinion was that I would be severely punished as soon as the sun rose.

I was trying to speak to the Commanders and make myself understood.

I was saying; "I was doing my duty", but it was in vain; I was getting a scolding from everybody. The Company Commander Mehmet Yıltay, who was my aunt's son, was so sad about the incidence but there was nothing to be done.

And the next day, there was great tension among everybody. Everyone was wondering, "What will happen". And in the afternoon, the curiosities were satisfied. A letter came from the Sanjak Headquarters (The office of the commander in chief of the Lefkoşa region) in order to be displayed on the notice boards in our company and all companies in Lefkoşa region.

The letter was describing how Süleyman Yusuf (there were no sur-names then) of the Support Company mujahids acted careful y and fulfilled his duty during his duty guard, and that the Commander decided to declare Süleyman Yusuf as a model mujahid, and to give him 5 Cyprus Pounds reward for this reason. My citation and 5 Cyprus Pounds reward were given to me on the following day at Lefkoşa Sanjak Headquarters. Everybody, including myself, was shocked. Nevertheless, both my commanders and I were honored.

The reward was also important because we, the student Mujahids, were given 5 Cyprus Pounds each month.

That is to say, the reward meant one month's salary for me. As soon as I received the money with the ceremony, I headed to the Company Headquarters, took off my uniform and dressed in civilian clothes. From there, I immediately passed to the Greek side from the Lokmacı check-point, and purchased a Jet brand green checkered jacket at a shop along the Ledra Street. It was exactly 5 Cyprus Pounds. I couldn't help looking at it for a long time but I was unable to find the money to buy it. It was too expensive. And now, that jacket was mine. Now, with my new jacket, I could show off at school and elsewhere.

Year 1969... I received a 5 Cyprus Pounds reward from the Commander... I immediately passed to the South, and bought the Jet brand green jacket that I am wearing in the photo, from the Ledra Street...

Ford Capri of the Manyera Family

And again, I am returning to this day. Still, the Bazooka is on my shoulder, and I am keeping an eye, straight ahead, and I keep waiting. Ersin is still not moving. I cannot choose but wait. And again the 1969-70's comes to my mind.

It was a very cold night. I am on guard duty of 01.00-04.00 in the small hours at the post we call Kırıkkale Back. I am thinking about finishing the duty and sleep at once. Because I had to be at school at 08:00 in the morning.

It was very cold during the guard duty. When I noticed the Ford Capri brand car that was parked just next to the guard post, I went and had a look. The car was not locked. In addition, the keys were on. I got in and sat down, and stayed there until the end of my guard. It was the car used by Ramiz Manyera, the well-known businessman.

After my guard duty, a couple of friends, who had just finished their guard duty, and I went and took the Ford Capri and started getting around. We weren't able to drive the car properly but we were very enthusiastic and taking pleasure in doing so. We were driving along the very narrow streets of the walled city of Lefkoşa. Then we went outside Lefkoşa and went up to Gönyeli.

We also passed by Gönyeli and turned back until we drove a further bit towards Boğaz.

I was driving the car and we were speeding. At one point, I lost control in a road bend at the exit of Gönyeli towards Lefkoşa, and having failed to take the bend, we had an accident. The car began rolling over, and it stopped upside down after tumbling three times. That beautiful car was shattered. Nevertheless, luckily we weren't hurt. We were three people.

A passerby in the first hours of the morning immediately picked and took us to the hospital, and the police was informed. We were examined at the first-aid department. Despite the car had tumbled three times, we were not hurt. The police arrived while we were going through examination at the hospital. Having quickly taken a brief statement from three of us, a policeman said "Let's go to the police station", and we left the hospital.

Before we went to the police station, we went by Mirata apartment building in Köşklüçiftlik. That is the location where our guard posts were situated and where we had taken the car. Ramiz Manyera was living in the Mirata apartment building. My friends and I, and the police sergeant, who was driving the car, were in the car. We stopped in front of the apartment building. The sergeant turned over to us and said "Children, sit here. I will go and inform Mr. Ramiz and come back"; having said so, he left.

Mr. Ramiz was a member of the Manyera family which was one of the well-established families of Cyprus. His father Niyazi Manyera was the first Health Minister of the Republic of Cyprus which was established in 1960. Mr. Ramiz was one of the Commanders of the Mujahids back in those years.

At the same time, he was the owner and director of the factory which used to produce various products including but not limited to Bel Cola, which was a Turkish Cypriot cola brand. He is particularly reputed to have had a very fast life in his youth. He was well-liked by the public due to his social relationships and personality.

We waited approximately 10 minutes in the car. Then the sergeant came.

He was confused a bit. He went on saying; "This Mr. Ramiz is a strange man.

I woke him up, told him the incident, and told him that his car was shattered.

And the man asked me, 'forget about the car, how are the kids, are the kids hurt?'" He added; "When I told him that nothing had happened to you, he was happy, and said "forget the car, don't do anything to the kids, and I have no complaints", hence he sent me away. "The Ford Capri had been smashed to bits, and the man couldn't care less. The man is strange."

And we went to the police station. After our statements had been taken, we were sent back to our company with my friends. There was astonishment also in the company. The commanders were in amazement because it was only one week ago that I had been declared as the role model mujahid and rewarded 5 Cyprus Pounds at Lefkoşa Commander. The commanders were saying

"The boy was tricked by the devil". Nevertheless, against all odds, I received punishment both during my military service and civil life, though they were minor. That's because the actual owner of the car was the then Chief Justice Ülfet Emin who was Mr. Ramiz's brother in law. This being the case, the police had to take a step further, and they did. However everybody was approaching thc casc by saying "thc kid has just given in to temptation and made a mistake".

And again I am back to the present time. The 89 mm rocket launcher is on my shoulder. My eye is on the scope, I am looking to the opposite position.

They are still shooting at another position nearby. There is still no movement from my friend Ersin. I am still waiting for the cooling period to be over and for the dud rocket in the rocket launcher to be replaced. And time hangs heavy on my hands.

And Fire

All of a sudden there is action on my right side. Ersin is doing something. At last, the cooling-off period is over, and Ersin is trying to remove the dud rocket and replace it with a new one. I, keeping my eye on the scope of the bazooka, keep on waiting. I think about the danger that in no time, the unexploded rocket may explode with delay; however there is nothing to be done. I think to myself; "We came to the end, hold your breath and wait".

In the meantime, the opposite fire has seized. No gun is being fired at us or to the adjacent position. But time hangs heavy on my hands. I am waiting for Ersin. And at last, Ersin softly touches my head. This means "you can fire".

And I, taking my courage in both hands, pull the trigger, keeping my eyes on the scope of the rocket launcher.

A terrific explosion and, at the same time, there is demolition and dust in the opposite position. Having watched this scene for a couple of seconds, suddenly the ceiling of the old building, which we were in, was not able to stand the pressure that emerged from the back of the rocket launcher during the shoot, and the ceiling made up of rafters tumbled down around us. But we were so lucky that the fallen rafters did not hurt any of us.

We urgently got out of the demolished building, and although we wanted to leave the place and return to our position at Ayios Kasiano; the Sergeant who was present there told us; "First go to the storehouse at the back of the Selimiye Mosque, and deliver the unexploded rocket, and then you can go to your positions."

The distance that we had to go was very close but there would be an unexploded rocket in our hands. But whatever will be, will be. Ersin and I took the rocket and left. We arrived at the warehouse in a couple of minutes. We found Tanju Cafer (Müezzinoğlu) there, and delivered the unexploded rocket to him, and let ourselves go.

When we returned to our position, everybody was anxious. Everybody, particularly who saw us covered with dust and dirt, were bombarding us with questions. And we were telling them everything down to the last detail and letting off steam.

Bottom line

And at the moment, all our prayers and efforts are directed for preventing these difficulties that our generation had faced from being faced by our grandchildren. Because the agonies suffered do not discriminate religion or race.

Printed in Dunstable, United Kingdom

67457033R00047